101
DOG TRAINING TIPS

Kirsten Mortensen

The Lyons Press

Guilford, Connecticut

An imprint of The Globe Pequot Press

To my daughter, Catharine

The Lyons Press is an imprint of The Globe Pequot Press.

10 9 8 7 6 5 4 3 2 1

Printed in the United States of America

Designed by Sheryl P. Kober

ISBN-13: 978-1-59228-921-9
ISBN-10: 1-59228-921-5

Library of Congress Cataloging-in-Publication Data is available on file.

To buy books in quantity for corporate use or incentives, call **(800) 962–0973, ext. 4551,** or e-mail **premiums@GlobePequot.com.**

Contents

Acknowledgments

Many thanks to Rochester, New York trainer Cindy Harrison of See Spot Think! Dog Training (www.seespotthink.net) for letting me take photographs of her students' dogs for this book.

Chapter 1

General Tips

Training a dog or puppy is a bit like solving a puzzle. Your dog's behavior is a blend of learned and instinctive behaviors. It's influenced by your dog's temperament, breeding, history, and of course by your training skills and techniques. The trick is to refine your training techniques so they accommodate your dog—and get results that are right for both of you.

As you do this, you'll find that you continually return to a few basic training concepts. The tips in this section cover these concepts to help strengthen all aspects of your training program.

If you focus on where you're going, you can keep a sense of perspective as you work with your dog.

tip 1. Focus on what you want—not what you don't want

If you don't know where you're going, how can you get there? That's true of most things in life, and it's true of dog training, too.

Sometimes we fall into the habit of thinking mostly about what we *don't* want. This happens a lot with dogs! We don't want our dog to pee in the house, or chew our shoes, or run away when we call, or bark like maniacs when our sweet old aunt comes to visit.

But think about it. Suppose you're about to adopt a puppy. Do you really want to spend the next ten, twelve, or fifteen years of your life chasing your dog around saying, "No no no"? Wouldn't it be better to guide your dog into behaviors that you want?

For example, instead of thinking, "I don't want my dog to chew the corners of my carpet," try, "I want my dog to chew his toys." Instead of, "I don't want my dog to jump up on my guests," how about, "I would like my dog to sit to greet people."

By framing your training goals in positive terms, you'll have a clear destination in mind. That's a great way to start your training journey.

Use rewards to reinforce the behaviors you are trying to train. If your dog loves to retrieve, a game of fetch is a great reward.

tip 2. Use rewards

One of the best things to happen in dog training in the past few years is the shift from emphasizing correction, or punishment, to emphasizing rewards.

Using rewards is a whole lot smarter for most trainers—and especially for companion dog owners. Perhaps the most important reason is that if you make a mistake using punishment, the consequences can be pretty sad. Some dogs—not all, but it can happen—may react to being punished by becoming aggressive or fearful. Other dogs shut down. They lose their sparkle. They may seem broken-spirited.

Many people also find that reward-based training *feels* better. It's nice to be a source of praise and treats, instead of a constant disciplinarian.

And best of all, reward-based training really works. That's because rewards help to nurture and strengthen behaviors we want in our dogs. If a behavior is rewarding, your dog is more likely to exhibit that behavior again in the future. By figuring out how to apply that simple rule, you can use rewards to reach virtually any training goal.

Kibble, cut up cheese, and cut up hot dog are examples of treats you can use to train. The pieces don't have to be big! Pea-sized treats are fine for most training.

tip 3. Try treats

Of all the rewards, treats are one of the most useful. They are versatile. You can use them at home, on walks, on trips, in public or private. They come in many varieties, which helps keep them fresh and interesting. Most important of all, dogs love food. For this reason, most dogs respond beautifully to being rewarded with treats.

Some people object to using treats. They think treats are like a bribe. But think about it: with bribes, the payment is demanded before the deal is finalized. When you train with treats, your dog earns those treats by giving you the behavior you're looking for. It's not a bribe—it's doggy payday!

While you can use people food as training treats, some foods are known or suspected to be toxic to dogs—including chocolate, grapes, raisins, and onions. Check with your vet if you're not sure about what training treats are safe.

Bonus tip: Keep treats small

While using treats to train is a great idea, you also have to watch your dog's calorie intake. The good news is treats don't have to be big to excite your dog. If you don't believe me, try spilling a few grains of rice under your table at the next mealtime—and then watch your dog help clean up. He'll go to great lengths to sniff out and lap up each grain of rice. That's the power of even tiny treats!

So don't think you need to use store-bought dog cookies or other treats for your training. I use tiny bits of kibble—the kind made for toy breed dogs—for much of my training needs. If you do buy or make larger treats, break them into pea-sized pieces for training.

You should also feed your dog less on days when you give a lot of training treats. Just make sure that the combination of treats and regular meals you're providing add up to a balanced diet. (Check with your vet on this if you're not sure!)

tip 4. Keep sessions short

Generally speaking, more frequent, shorter training sessions are more effective than less frequent, longer sessions.

How short is short? This depends, in part, on your dog. If you notice your dog starting to lose interest, the training session has already lasted too long.

A good rule of thumb is to work on something for three to five repetitions at a time. Then take a break. Play with your dog, or do something else for a while—then come back later for another (short) session.

tip 5. Be patient

One of the biggest challenges with training a dog is expecting perfection—especially when you expect it right away. We often have a mental image of how a well-trained dog behaves. But training dogs takes time, so be patient. You and your dog will be together for a number of years. If you don't reach all of your training goals the first couple of weeks, that's okay. You'll get there.

To train complex behaviors, break them down into pieces. For example, training your dog to give—let you take an object from her mouth—is an important piece of a retrieve.

tip 6. Break behaviors into manageable pieces

Many behaviors are actually made up of more than one action or position: they are several behaviors, combined. For example, paying attention is a foundation behavior for recall (coming when called). For a dog to come when called, she has to notice that you've called her. So the first "piece" of the recall behavior is getting your dog to pay attention to you. If you want your dog to retrieve a ball or toy when you toss it, one part of the behavior you need to train is *give*—she has to let you take the ball from her mouth. *Sit* is a component of the sit/stay behavior.

Sometimes we need to invest time in mastering pieces of a more complex behavior before we can move on to the behavior itself.

Think of training your dog as a kind of dance. First you learn the steps. Then you put them together into the final routine. By breaking the behavior into its smaller steps, your training will be more successful. It will also be easier to notice how much progress you're making.

When dogs are excited by something—like a squirrel in the backyard—it can be hard to get and keep their attention. So pick a place with few distractions for training, especially when you are working on a new behavior.

tip 7. Manage distractions

Distractions—that is, anything that competes for your dog's attention—can complicate your training regimen. So it's important that you manage them.

For example, take a behavior like sitting. You might think that a sit is a sit whether you expect it in your kitchen, at the park, or on a crowded street.

But it's not the same. Some environments have a lot of distractions. Some have few. Some distractions are . . . very distracting. Maybe your dog sits beautifully whenever you are in your living room and you say, "Sit." Maybe he'll even sit beautifully for you when you are outside in your backyard. That doesn't mean he'll sit when you ask him to just as a squirrel runs by.

So here's the thing. When you start training a behavior, pick a place that doesn't have many distractions. Think boring. Later, as your dog becomes more fluent in the behavior, you can try it in situations where there are more distractions.

By managing the distractions as part of your training, your dog's behaviors will have a solid foundation. When you do introduce distractions, he'll be better prepared to handle them.

Something interesting has caught this dog's attention. Notice the pricked ears, the position of the tail, and the alert expression of the eyes.

tip 8. Observe your dog

Every dog is different. To figure out how to train your dog, you have to become a good observer. Is your dog relaxed? Aroused? Is it easy to get his attention, or hard? What rewards get him jazzed?

The more closely you watch your dog, the more information you have about whether your training is working. You'll be better able to adjust your training so that it fits *your* dog.

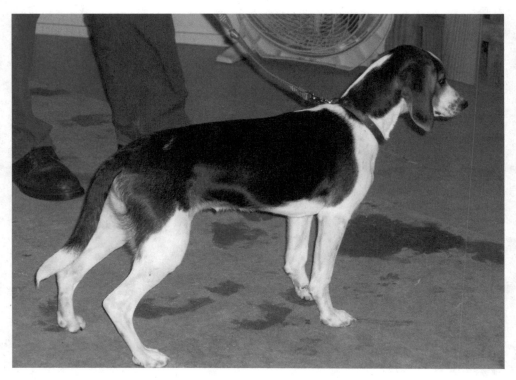

This dog is fairly relaxed and not paying attention to anything in particular. Note the position of the ears and tail.

Dogs communicate through body language. A play bow is a dog's way of enticing other dogs—or people—to join in a romp. (It can also be a cute "trick" to put on cue!)

tip 9. Take notes

What works with your dog? What doesn't? Have you really made progress in your training program? What have you tried in the past, and how well did it work?

Training your dog isn't just about your dog: it's also about you. And sometimes the best way to become a better trainer is to take notes. That way you have a record you can refer to. You also have a way of checking your progress as a trainer.

Notes may also help you understand your dog's behavior—and that can sometimes help you improve your training.

Suppose you decide you'd like your dog to bark less. Begin by recording when your dog barks. Doing this may help you uncover a pattern. Maybe, for example, you discover your dog barks more on weekends than on weekdays. You think about it some more and realize that you are more "up" and excited on weekends. There may be more activity around your home as well. If this is the case, your dog may be responding to the extra excitement by barking more. So now you can come up with a solution. Perhaps you work on reinforcing calmer behaviors. Maybe you try to be more relaxed yourself. Maybe you work on keeping your dog more low-key when greeting guests.

Taking notes also means that if you ever consult with a professional trainer or behaviorist, you're not relying entirely on memory. The information you provide is more likely to be factual—which will help you both get to a solution that works.

tip 10. Be consistent

Dogs learn fastest when we're consistent.

If you're trying to train a behavior, make sure you reward it consistently. If you've made a rule for your dog, don't ever break it. For example, if you are training your dog to sit when she greets you, make sure you never reward her (by paying attention to her, for instance) when she jumps up.

tip 11. Learn a little theory

With dogs, what you *do* is most important. You can know everything there is to know about dog behavior and training—but if you don't actually work with your dog, all that knowledge isn't going to help you a bit.

And yet, it is useful to know a little theory. Why? Because your dog is unique. No trainer has ever worked with *your* dog. No writer has ever written a book about *your* dog. Theory can help you come up with creative ideas and solutions, even when your dog's behavior doesn't quite fit anyone else's experience.

So take the time to learn a little behavioral theory. Then, if your dog does something that *seems* really strange, you'll be better prepared to understand it, why it happened, and how you should respond.

(Many of the books I've listed in Additional Reading can help you learn some behavioral theory.)

tip 12. Learn a little body language!

It's also helpful to learn how to read a dog's body language. We like to think we know our dogs, and that we can empathize with our dogs. But the fact is, we can't *really* get into a dog's brain and experience what a dog experiences.

But we can observe dogs. And we can come to reasonable conclusions about their general states, such as whether they are relaxed or aroused. These observations, in turn, can help make us better trainers. They can help us understand how our training is going.

For example, if my dog becomes too aroused, she's more difficult to train. It can be hard for me to even get her attention. By watching her body language, I can adjust my expectations and avoid setting her up for training failures.

Dogs who are aroused may have raised hackles. Their ears will be pricked. They may hold their tails erect.

A dog who is anxious may hold his tail between his legs. He may crouch or "slink" along the floor. He may turn his head away from whatever is making him anxious.

Every dog is different. The better we become at reading our dog's responses to our training and to the environment, the better trainers we become.

Every dog is unique. As you learn your dog's body language, you'll become a more skilled trainer.

tip 13. Don't be afraid to ask for help

Sometimes, it helps to get advice from someone who has been around a lot of dogs. This might be a friend or acquaintance whose judgment you trust. In other cases, it may be helpful to consult a professional: a veterinarian, professional dog trainer, or a behaviorist. An obvious example is if your dog snaps or bites, or exhibits some other behavior that frightens you.

If your dog's behavior or temperament suddenly changes for no apparent reason, a trip to the vet is always a good idea. You may discover that your dog has a medical condition, or she is in pain for some reason and that is causing her to act differently.

Or maybe you just need a little help solving a training or behavior problem. We all get stumped sometimes! Talking with someone who can offer a fresh perspective may be exactly what you need to get your training program back on track.

This dog is alert but relaxed. His eyes are alert, but his lips and ears are relaxed, and he is lying on one hip, rather than in a "sphinx down"—or as I used to call it with my last dog, launch position.

Enrolling your dog in a training class can be beneficial for several reasons. Your instructor can critique your training technique and pass along his or her knowledge. It also gives you a chance to practice behaviors around other dogs—a major distraction.

tip 14. Never stop learning!

One of the reasons training dogs is so much fun is that there's always room for improvement. So keep reading, researching, and talking to people who have dogs or train dogs. The more you learn, the better you'll get at training your dog.

Chapter 2

Good Dog Manners

Most dogs today spend a lot of time with us in our homes. This section gives you tips for working on behaviors, including some basic obedience, that will help keep your indoor time together pleasant and manageable.

Be sure to reward your dog, sometimes, when he's simply relaxing. Reinforcing calm behavior can help your dog become a more pleasant companion.

tip 15. Calm is good

Picture two dogs. One is tearing around the house, barking like mad, and jumping up on people and furniture. The other dog is sitting quietly and looking at you. Which is the "good dog"?

Most of us would choose dog #2. Does that mean we don't want our dogs to be spirited and excited some of the time? No, of course not. But for most of us, most of the time, a calm dog is a better companion.

So in addition to all the other training you do, make sure you reinforce calm behavior. This can be tricky, because we tend to notice our dogs when they are calling attention to themselves. But you know what? If you ignore your dog when he's doing nothing—but then get all excited and chase him around the house when he walks up to you with your shoe in his mouth—you may be training him to be a troublemaker!

So be sure to praise and pet your dog when he's quiet and calm. Give him a treat, now and then, when he's lying quietly or snoozing.

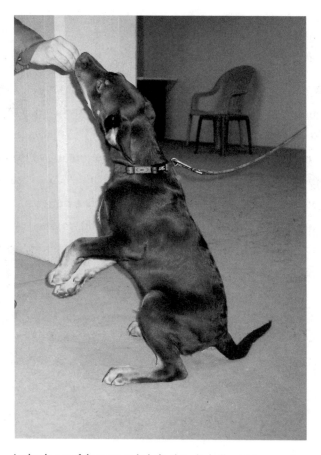

Luring is a useful way to train behaviors, including tricks as well as standard obedience behaviors.

tip 16. Use basic obedience as a behavior foundation

People have all different goals for their dogs. Some of us are looking for companion animals while others will involve their dogs in competitions, such as agility or obedience.

Regardless of your goals, it's a good idea to do some basic obedience with your dog. When you have some foundation behaviors on cue—things like sit and down—you'll be able to manage your dog a little better. Basic obedience also builds a connection between you and your dog.

So even if all you want is a buddy to join you for walks and curl up with you on the couch when you relax, plan to do a little basic obedience.

To lure a sit, hold a treat over your dog's head and move your hand backward until he drops into the sit position.

Almost there! As soon as this fellow has both front paws on the floor, he gets his treat.

tip 17. Begin with sit or down

Sit and *down* are two great basic obedience behaviors. They come fairly naturally to dogs (dogs sit and lie down all the time), and they are behaviors you can train indoors, which is a relatively low-distraction environment.

Sit and down are also useful in a lot of different situations. For instance, telling your dog to sit when greeting human visitors is a great behavior to instill in your dog. Telling your dog, "Down" is a way to keep your dog's mouth away from your kid's peanut butter and jelly sandwich when she's eating on the couch. In fact, you can use either sit or down as an "alternative behavior" any time you want your dog to *not* do something else.

An easy way to train sit or down is luring. With luring, you use a treat to "lure" your dog's body into the desired position.

The basic procedure for luring is to close a treat in your fist. Your dog will be able to smell it, but not see it or eat it (until you're ready). Then move your hand in a way that gets your dog to take the position you're trying to train. When she's in the right position, say, "Yes" and give her the treat.

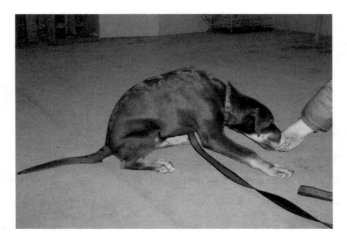

To lure a down, use a treat to draw your dog's nose toward the floor.

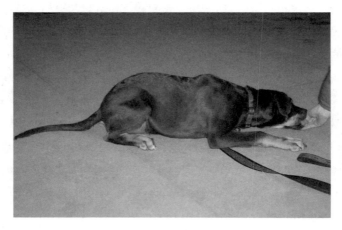

He's there! Say, "Yes!" and let him take the treat!

For example, to train a sit, begin with your dog standing. Holding the treat in your fist, move your hand back over the dog's head, as if you are petting her. As her nose follows your hand, she'll drop into a sit. Say, "Yes!"—and give her the treat.

Do this four more times. Then take a break for a while. Practicing four or five times, per session, is plenty. In fact, most dogs do better with frequent, short training sessions than with long sessions.

In your next training sessions, you'll notice your dog catching on: she'll start sitting faster. She may even sit as soon as she realizes that you have a treat in your hand. When this happens, don't lure her any more—just give her the treat.

At that point, you can start to add the sit cue. As you see her begin to sit, say, "Sit." Then give her the treat. Again, repeat this four or five times, per training session.

What you'll notice next is that saying, "sit" triggers the sit behavior. Congratulations! You are now on the way to having your dog's sit behavior on cue.

Training your dog to lie down uses the same process, only instead of luring your dog into a sit, put your hand all the way down on the floor so that you draw her into the down position.

tip 18. **Make it harder—a little at a time**

It's one thing for your dog to sit on cue in the kitchen, when there's nobody else around and he knows you have a treat in your hand. But you may need your dog to respond to cues like sit in other situations, too. So it's a good idea to work on these behaviors under more difficult conditions.

For example, most dogs are more distracted outside than inside. So work on having your dog sit in your yard, or during walks. You may also work on these behaviors when there are other people or animals around. If your dog becomes excited by doorbells or telephones ringing, for example, use these events to add a little more challenge to your training.

At the same time, don't set your expectations too high. It's far better to take baby steps than ask too much of your dog, too quickly.

Suppose your dog sits reliably, on cue, in the house. A logical next step would be to work on sitting in a quiet yard. If you take your dog to a busy city street and ask for a sit, he may be too overwhelmed by all that's going on around him to respond. But if you focus on a reliable sit in your backyard for a few weeks, tackling sitting on a busy city sidewalk is more likely to succeed.

And of course, every dog is different! Some dogs get distracted more easily than others. So make sure you're paying attention to how quickly your dog catches on when you add distractions—including how easy or hard it is to get his attention. Then adjust the speed of your training program to your dog.

tip 19. Practice!

So what's next? Practice! Do numerous repetitions. Practice in different rooms of the house. Practice when your dog knows you're holding a treat—and when she knows you're not. Vary the reward.

In a "macaroni down," a dog flops over onto one hip. Dogs in this position can't get up as quickly as they can in a "sphinx down," so it's a good training goal if you want your dog to settle in one spot after you ask for a down.

Sometimes reward a sit with a treat. Sometimes reward it with pets and praise, or by playing a game.

Don't make your practice sessions long, but do practice often. If you take a few minutes, every day, to work with your dog, you'll make steady progress toward your goals.

In a "sphinx down," a dog can jump again quickly.

One behavior you should consider training is, "Go to your bed." This is very helpful for your dog's indoor manners!

tip 20. Use obedience skills for control and focus

Once your dog knows a few basic obedience skills, you can use those behaviors to ask your dog to control herself, and to focus her attention.

For instance, suppose you are taking your dog on a leash walk and a squirrel runs by. Assuming you've worked on a sit outdoors—while walking on leash, with enticing distractions nearby—you now have a tool to keep your dog from going crazy about the squirrel.

You can use your dog's obedience training to manage your dog—to prevent her from getting too close to people if they aren't dog lovers, or if you aren't certain they will approach your dog properly. Having your dog sit or lie down on cue is also very useful around small children—particularly if they are carrying food!

If your dog tends to become anxious or aroused, asking for a sit or down can help redirect her attention, and may help her become more calm.

tip 21. Use sit or down when going through doors

It can be annoying, or even dangerous, to have a dog that bolts out of an open door. So use the sit or down behavior to make sure your dog waits until you are ready for him to go outside.

tip 22. To prevent begging, don't feed from the table

Because food is so rewarding, if you feed your dog while you're eating, guess what—she's going to reappear the next time you're eating, hoping for a repeat performance.

So if you don't want your dog to beg, you need to resist temptation. You need to set a rule that you'll never toss tidbits from your plate—and then you need to stick to it. Consistency is very important. Break your rule once and all your good training flies out of the window. (This assumes you never drop food accidentally while you're eating, as I've been known to do; but that's an entirely different story!)

If you have a dog that jumps, make sure you don't reward it. Withdraw your attention by turning your back. This helps train him to sit during greetings.

tip 23. Turn your back to teach polite greeting

When dogs greet someone, having their greeting reciprocated is very rewarding. You can use that as a way to train polite greeting behavior: simply ignore your dog until she sits. Only when she sits do you reward her by paying attention to her.

To make this even more effective, quickly turn your back on her any time she jumps up. If you do this consistently, most dogs will catch on very quickly that they need to sit to get a hello and all that nice petting.

tip 24. Ask guests to turn their backs

Make sure you also instruct your guests to turn their backs on your dog unless he sits. Dogs are smart. They'll learn to greet different people different ways—depending on what works. So train your guests. With their help, you'll make great progress in encouraging your dog to greet people politely.

If your dog isn't trained, yet, to greet people politely, leash her when someone comes to the door. This gives you more control and can prevent bad habits from getting established.

tip 25. Leash your dog

This is a tip for when you have visitors come to your home.

One of the challenges with training polite greetings is keeping bad habits from getting started. If you have a puppy, or a dog who is particularly rambunctious, try leashing him during greetings. Then stand some distance from the new visitors—and don't go any closer unless your dog has all four feet on the floor.

This uses the greeting itself as a reward. If your dog has all four feet on the floor, take a step closer to the guest. If he rears up, take a step (or several if needed) away. Then step closer again—but again, only if your dog keeps all four feet on the floor.

If you follow this procedure carefully, and consistently refuse to let your dog approach a visitor unless he has four on the floor, you'll be surprised at how quickly he catches on.

tip 26. Be calm during greetings

Dogs pick up cues from us on how to behave. If you are calm during greetings, you'll help your dog stay calmer as well.

Pay attention to your body language and tone of voice as you greet your dog. Relaxed, quiet movements and a soft, lower-pitched voice can help keep your dog from becoming overly excited.

And don't initiate high-energy play when you first return after an absence. Wait for a half hour or so, then play.

tip 27. Reward a polite greeting

To a dog, greeting is a reward in itself. But you can make that reward even more reinforcing by adding other things your dogs likes. For example, suppose you enter your house or apartment. Your dog rushes up to say hi. You ask for a sit and your dog sits. In addition to greeting and petting him, you might also give him a treat. Or toss him a favorite toy you keep near the door.

tip 28. Arrange greeting practice sessions

To work on greeting behaviors, set up practice sessions. To work on how your dog greets you, go in and out of the door four or five times. Ask for a sit on each greeting and reward your dog when he greets you politely.

To work on how your dog greets guests, arrange for a friend to come to your home as a pretend guest. Doorbells and people knocking often serve as triggers that get a dog excited; so with this kind of practice session, you can also work on rewarding your dog for responding more calmly when someone comes to the door.

tip 29. **Train your dog to drop it**

It's a good idea to train your dog so he'll let you take something from his mouth. To do this, teach your dog that when he gives something up, he gets something even better.

Start by putting together some treats that your dog really likes. Then give your dog a toy to hold in his mouth. Pick a toy that isn't his favorite, or one that he's been playing with a lot lately (so he's a bit bored with it). When he's holding the toy in his mouth, offer him the treat. Since he can't take the treat with something else in his mouth, chances are pretty good that he'll drop the toy. Say, "Yes," pick up the toy, and give him the treat. Then give him the toy back.

Make sure you always pick the toy up before you give him the treat. That way, he won't learn to take the treat from you and then lunge for the toy again.

And always give him the toy back, too, as you practice this behavior. Doing so shows him that dropping it doesn't mean he's losing. It means he's getting two things: the treat *and* the toy.

After five repetitions, take a break, and repeat a little later.

Very quickly, you'll notice that he doesn't wait for you to offer the treat. He'll drop the toy right away. When this happens, it's time to add the cue. As he drops the toy, say, "Drop it." Then pick the toy up, give him the treat, and hand back the toy.

Once you've practiced this awhile, make the game a little harder. Say, "Drop it" when he doesn't know you have treats nearby.

Once he reacts to the drop it cue consistently, you have a tool to use for times when your dog picks up things you'd rather he didn't— like a shoe or something smelly he found out in the yard. Of course, if he's got your shoe in his mouth, you aren't going to give it back after you give him a treat. Just make the treat something extra special.

tip 30. Teach your dog not to worry about his dinner bowl

Sometimes, dogs exhibit a behavior called *resource guarding*: they become aggressive toward people (or other dogs) who get too close to something the dog values.

Resource guarding is one of those behaviors that is better prevented than cured. So if you get a dog as a puppy, start working right away to prevent him from guarding his food dish. Teach him that any time you reach for it, something wonderful is going to happen. For instance, suppose you normally feed your puppy kibble. From time to time, walk up to your puppy while he's eating and drop a piece of something wonderful in his dish, like a piece of hot dog, roast chicken, or liver, or a dab of canned tuna.

This shows your puppy that when your hands come near his dish, it's not because you're going to take his food away. It's because you're going to give him something even better. If you have other people in your family, have them play this same game with your puppy.

If you adopt an older dog, you can try the same technique, but proceed with caution. If you observe any signs of aggression (such as growling, baring teeth, snapping, nipping, or biting) you should consult a behaviorist or experienced trainer to put together a behavior modification program that will keep you safe.

Bonus tip: Trade up toys, too.

Practice showing your dog that when you take toys away, it means good things, also. Give your dog a toy she doesn't care about as much. Take it from her, then immediately hand her a favorite toy.

Chapter 3

Housetraining

For most people, having a housetrained dog is a high training priority. The tips in this chapter will help you understand the basics of guiding your dog to develop desirable pottying behaviors.

tip 31. Start immediately

Get started on housetraining the first few minutes a new dog comes into your home. One of the secrets of good pottying behavior is to establish habits. If you don't start reinforcing good pottying habits with your dog right away—the very first day she comes to your home—you're making the job harder than it should be. The last thing you want is to let your dog get into the habit of pottying where she shouldn't.

tip 32. Prevent "accidents"

The better you are at preventing accidents, the more quickly your dog will become housetrained.

So how do you prevent housetraining accidents? First, make sure you give your dog frequent bathroom breaks. (If he's a very young puppy, this may mean taking him outside every couple of hours at first.)

Second, pay attention to your dog's behavior. Many dogs act a certain way when they need to relieve themselves. They may whine, go to the door, or circle around the floor sniffing. Puppies often need a bathroom break right after playing, eating, or napping.

And finally, consider a crate for those times when you can't directly supervise your dog. In most cases, confining your dog to his sleeping area trains him to wait to relieve himself.

There are several types of crates. This model is a wire crate.
(Photo courtesy of Doskocil Manufacturing Company, Inc.)

This type of crate can also be used for safely transporting your dog.
(Photo courtesy of Doskocil Manufacturing Company, Inc.)

tip 33. Use a crate

Crates are a great housetraining tool. Healthy dogs don't usually soil their own beds. So confining your dog to her bed when you can't directly supervise her is a great way to prevent housetraining accidents.

Of course, it's important to introduce your dog to the crate properly. Your dog should view her crate as a comfortable place where she wants to be when she's resting or sleeping. Research crate-training or work with a professional trainer if you have any questions about getting your dog used to a crate.

tip 34. Don't punish accidents

Punishing a dog for housetraining mistakes has the potential to back-fire. Your dog doesn't understand why she shouldn't pee on the rug. It may seem like a perfectly fine toilet to her! So if you punish her, you may think you're training her not to pee on the rug. But what you might actually be teaching her is to mistrust you—to run away when she notices certain body language, or hears a certain tone of voice. You may end up training her to pee when you're not around. Or to pick a spot you won't notice for a while.

So, as strange as it may sound, if your dog has an accident, don't try to correct her. Take a deep breath, clean it up, and resolve to do a better job supervising the pup, from now on.

tip 35. Clean up right away!

If your dog does have an accident, it's important to get rid of the smell—or he might decide to use that spot again.

Keep a cleaner on hand that is made to get rid of pet odors. This type of cleaner uses enzymes that chemically break down urine or other organic waste. You can find these products at pet supply stores, supermarkets, and department stores.

If your dog does potty indoors, clean up right away using a product that breaks down the stain chemically. (Photo courtesy of Eight in One Pet Products.)

First blot up as much of the accident as you can, then follow the directions on the container to finish the job. Keep your dog away from the spot until it is fully dry.

Bonus tip: Keep a careful watch

Your best tools for housetraining are your two eyes. Until your dog is reliably housetrained, don't leave him alone. The pottying habits he establishes on his own may not be the ones you want.

---

tip 36. Reward appropriate pottying

When your dog does go where you want him to go—let him know. Give him treats. Praise him! Give him the one-on-one attention that he adores. Throw a ball or Frisbee for him. The more you associate proper pottying with good stuff, the faster your dog will develop those great pottying habits.

tip 37. Cue it!

Yup, believe it or not, you can train your dog to go on cue. First, pick the cue you want to use. Some people use separate cues for urinating and defecating. You could say, "Go pee" and "Go poo," or "Number one" and "Number two," or choose something more discrete, like "Hurry up" or "Go now."

Once you've picked your cue, say it every time your dog starts to do her business. Do this consistently, and your cue will be able to trigger the behavior. So when you're in a hurry, and it's pouring down rain, you'll have an extra trick up your sleeve to get your dog to finish.

tip 38. Pick a potty spot

Think about where you want your dog to potty, and focus your training on getting her to go in that spot. Here are some things to consider as you choose your dog's potty spot.

- You may sometimes want or need to supervise your dog when she relieves herself, so the spot shouldn't be too far away or difficult to get to.

- The spot should be away from places where people need to walk.

- Cleaning up after your dog is easier on some surfaces than others. For instance, my dog's potty spot is under some evergreen trees along the edge of my lawn. Picking up off the layer of dead needles on the ground is really easy!

tip 39. Schedule a puppy's meals to help prevent accidents

If you let your puppy drink too much right before bed, you make it much harder for her to get through the night without a housetraining accident. The same goes for meals. Eating can stimulate a puppy to eliminate. Feed your puppy right before bedtime and you raise the likelihood that she'll need to go out again before morning.

Of course you have to make sure your puppy has plenty of water, so give her access to water during the day. But put the water dish away an hour or two before bedtime. And schedule your puppy's last meal of the day earlier in the evening as well.

tip 40. Potty first—walk later

Dogs can be very tricky sometimes. They can learn to train us! For example, suppose you combine your dog's walks with his bathroom breaks. You get home from work, leash him, and take him outdoors. You walk a bit, he relieves himself—and as soon as he does, you head back home.

Well, guess what? For most dogs, walks are highly rewarding. So by following this pattern, you may inadvertently teach your dog that pottying means the walk is over—and your clever dog may just learn to put off relieving himself for as long as possible!

But suppose you turn this around and make the walk a reward for him getting his business out of the way? Here's how you do it: instead of setting out for your walk first thing, begin your outing with a bathroom break. Leash your dog. Wait until he relieves himself. Then start your walk.

If you do this, you are using the walk to reward fast pottying behavior. You'll have a dog who does his business quickly—and you are in charge when it comes to the length of the walk.

Chapter 4

When Your Dog's Alone

Dogs are social animals. However, many people work outside of their homes, leaving their dogs alone for several hours during the day. While most dogs adjust to this arrangement and accept it as part of their routine, some dogs do not. If your dog gets into mischief while left alone, he might be suffering from boredom, or he might find being alone stressful. Use the tips in this book to prevent separation problems and to help alleviate problematic behaviors triggered by your dog being left alone.

tip 41. Prepare for separations

If your work schedule means you'll be leaving your dog alone for some period of time on a regular basis, it's a good idea to prepare your dog.

For instance, when you adopt a new puppy or dog, try to arrange some practice separations during your first few days together. As you introduce your dog into your routine, leave him alone, periodically, for varying lengths of time. This helps get him used to the fact that you'll be apart sometimes.

Dogs shouldn't be left unsupervised with certain toys. My dog loves to chew rope toys, but when they start to fall apart, I take them away so that she won't swallow any long pieces of string.

tip 42. Give your dog things to do

Some dogs have problems being left alone because they get bored. So find ways to keep your dog busy while you're out.

One option is to leave toys with your dog. Make sure the toy itself will withstand unsupervised chewing without coming apart! You want your dog to be safe while you're not home.

Some chew toys are hollow inside so that you can fill them with food or treats. Working the food free helps keep your dog occupied. A variation on this idea is a puzzle-style toy. For example, look for hollow toys designed so that bits of kibble fall out if the toy is rolled around.

Hiding treats around the house is another way to give your dog a problem to solve when you're not home.

Puzzle-style toys dispense treats when your dog plays with them. They can keep a dog occupied when you're away or busy doing other things.

Some dog toys are designed so that you can stuff them with treats. Dogs love to spend time working the food free. (Photo courtesy of Kong Company.)

tip 43. Consider a sitter

If you are regularly away for many hours at a time, consider hiring someone to come to your home to take your dog for a walk and give him some attention.

Bonus tip: A crate is a tool, not a crutch

If you have crate-trained your dog, you might be tempted to simply confine a dog who becomes destructive when you're not home.

While this can work as a short-term fix, it doesn't really address the underlying issues that caused the behavior in the first place. If your dog is bored, for instance, or becomes distressed when left alone for too long, putting him in a crate won't help alleviate the boredom or distress.

The crate is a great tool for keeping your dog safe and happy when you aren't there to supervise him. But it's not a substitute for giving your dog the quality of life that he needs and deserves.

---

tip 44. Keep good-byes low-key

Your dog takes cues from you. If you signal that good-byes aren't a big deal, your dog is more likely to accept periods of separation. So don't fuss over your dog right before you're leaving. Arrange it so that your dog is occupied with something—maybe a food-stuffed chew toy. Then leave when she's not paying attention to you.

tip 45. Get help for extreme anxiety

Dogs are individuals. Some dogs handle being alone with no problems whatsoever. Other dogs might react to being left alone with some mildly undesirable behavior—maybe getting into a little mischief, chewing something she shouldn't, or a bit of barking or whining.

But with some dogs, these behaviors can escalate to the point where the dog becomes destructive, injures herself, or creates problems with neighbors. If this is the case, consult a trainer, behaviorist, or your veterinarian for additional options.

Chapter 5

Trips to the Vet and Beyond

Most of us need to take our dogs on trips with us, at least once in a while. And every dog is going to have to visit a veterinarian on a regular basis. Here are some tips to help keep trips with your dog safe and comfortable, whether your destination is a vacation paradise or that yearly checkup.

tip 46. Safety first

People today recognize that wearing seat belts saves lives. Dogs need to be kept safe during car rides as well. One option is a crate. Choose a crate that is designed for transporting dogs and sized properly for your dog. And make sure you strap or tie it securely so the crate won't bounce or slide around if you have to stop suddenly or encounter some other incident.

Using a crate while traveling with your dog not only keeps your dog safe, it also helps ensure that emergency personnel would be able to move your dog if you ever needed help during a road trip.

You can also find special doggy seat belts. These are typically harnesses that attach to the car seat belt. If you do try a harness, introduce it to your dog in a relaxed way, giving him lots of treats and pets so that he associates the harness with rewards.

Lifting your dog into a car isn't always practical, and letting your dog jump in and out of a car or truck might not be safe for the dog. So consider using a ramp (this one is manufactured by Petmate) to help your dog get in and out of vehicles. (Photo courtesy of Doskocil Manufacturing Company Inc.)

tip 47. Practice making trips happy!

Make sure your dog associates trips with good things. For example, as you load up the car for a road trip, give your dog plenty of pets and praise—plus treats, if they don't upset her tummy. Do the same if you are taking your dog on an airplane or other vehicle.

If permitted, give your dog a safe chew toy to give her an outlet for her energy during the trip.

One mistake people sometimes make is when they only take their dogs in the car when it's time to go to the vet. This can be a problem if your dog doesn't like vet exams. If your dog dislikes vet visits, make sure you occasionally take your dog on rides that don't end at the vet's office (then read the next section for tips on making trips to the vet more rewarding).

tip 48. On vet trips, make the positive outweigh the negative

Veterinarians and their staff poke and prod. They deliver vaccinations and sometimes oral medications. They expect dogs to do things, like stand on high metal tables, which may seem strange or upsetting.

Your job is to make sure lots of nice things happen, too. What does your dog find most rewarding? Find ways to incorporate rewarding experiences into your vet visits. That way, the dog will associate trips to the vet with positive, instead of negative, experiences.

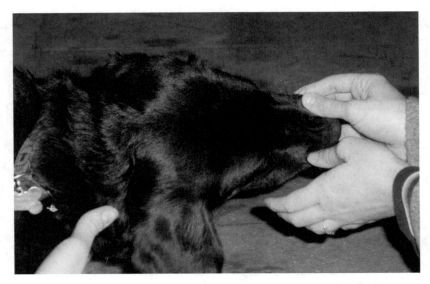

To get your dog ready for vet visits, practice handling her muzzle. Be sure to give her frequent treats as you practice. She'll learn to associate having her teeth and gums examined with positive things.

tip 49. Get your dog used to being handled

Give your dog plenty of at-home practice being handled the way veterinary professionals handle dogs. Pretend you're giving her an examination. Touch and hold your dog's feet. Look in her ears. Combine your "exam" with lots of pets and treats so that your dog learns that being handled that way is fun and pleasant.

tip 50. Remember your treats on trips to the vet

A great way to make a trip to a vet a positive experience is to bring along some treats. Feed them to your dog throughout the visit. You might also want to have the veterinary staff offer treats as well.

tip 51. Don't be afraid to switch vets

Veterinarians are human. Each handles their canine patients a little differently. Not every dog is going to do well with a given vet.

You are your dog's protector and advocate. If you suspect your vet isn't a good match for your dog, find a new vet who is able to make exams a more positive experience for your dog.

When it comes to walking your dog, your training goal is a loose leash.

Chapter 6

Leash Walking

Most of us need to walk with our dogs on leash, at least occasionally. And if walks are your dog's primary outlet for exercise, you'll be taking your dog out on a leash every day.

For this reason, it's important to train your dog to walk safely and calmly while leashed. The goal is a loose leash, meaning that during leash walks, your dog doesn't pull or strain. Here are some tips to help.

Reinforce polite leash walking by delivering food rewards when your dog is in a heel position.

tip 52. Reward the right position

The main thing you need to do to train a loose leash is reward your dog for staying in a position that is close enough to you that the leash isn't taut. Food treats are a great tool for this: anytime your dog is walking nicely—the leash is loose—say, "Yes" and give your dog a treat.

If your dog puts pressure on the leash, stop and wait for her to look at you and come closer to you again. When she does that, say, "Yes" and give her a treat.

You can also use the yes/treat combination when your dog glances at you during the walk. Doing that is a nice way to reinforce her "checking in" to see where you are.

tip 53. Start indoors

Most of us think of leash walking as an outdoor behavior. But for most dogs, the best place to start learning is inside. That's because indoors is a relatively low-distraction environment. You won't be competing with as many things for your dog's attention. He'll be more likely to notice the rewards you're offering for nice leash behaviors.

tip 54. When you do go outside, pick a boring spot

As you progress in your loose leash training indoors, you'll eventually be ready to move outside. Outside is a higher-distraction environment—but you can find ways to make the transition from low- to high-distraction a little more gradual. Try to find the most boring places you can. For example, your next step, after indoor practice, might be walking in your driveway, or in the backyard. The sidewalk closest to your home or apartment is probably more boring than the park.

If you have a fenced-in yard, you might try letting your dog out loose first, so she has a chance to check all the new smells or sights that weren't there the last time she was out. Then snap on the leash for some walking practice.

tip 55. **Progress slowly**

Leash walking, like any outdoor behavior, is challenging because outside is distracting. Outside, a dog's senses are being tickled by myriad sounds, sights, and smells. We sometimes forget that we're asking a lot when we expect our dogs to notice what *we* want when there is so much other, interesting stuff going on!

Of course, every dog is different. Some dogs will naturally be calmer, and some will be more excitable. The trick is to match your training program to your dog. If you are consistently "failing" in your attempts to get your dog to walk nicely on leash, you've been trying to progress too quickly. Go back to the beginning and start over—and this time, make sure your dog has mastered the baby steps before moving on.

tip 56. Use the walk as a reward

One of the best rewards you have for training loose leash walking is the walk itself. Your dog wants to *go*. So make moving forward a reward for a loose leash.

Conversely, if your dog ever puts pressure on the leash—if he ever makes the leash taut—then stop. Wait for him to look at you. Wait for him to take a step back toward you so that the leash goes slack again. When he does that, start walking again.

If you do this consistently, your dog will learn that he makes *you* go by keeping the leash loose.

If you want your dog to keep the leash slack, never reward him when he's put tension on the leash.

tip 57. Avoid bad habits

If you let your dog practice pulling, guess what? You're training your dog to pull. If your dog hasn't mastered loose leash walking, find alternative ways to give her exercise, such as romps in a fenced-in yard. Don't rely on leash walks for her daily exercise until she's had plenty of practice keeping that lead loose.

tip 58. Consider training tools

There are a number of tools—special harnesses, head harnesses, and collars—designed to help people train their dogs to walk nicely on leash. Each tool has its advocates. Before you choose a leash walking tool, however, it's important to ask yourself how the tool works. As with all training techniques, choose a leash training tool that reinforces your dog's best qualities—such as confidence, calmness, and self-control.

Premiere Pet Products is a reliable source for tools to help train loose leash walking. I have been very pleased with their Easy Walk Harness, pictured here. (Photo courtesy of Premiere Pet Products, LLC.)

It's also important to use these training tools correctly. Proper fit is very important. Stop using the tool if you suspect it is hurting your dog, or making her feel intimidated or anxious—because setting up your dog to have those kinds of responses could lead to more serious problems later.

Another Premiere leash training tool is their Gentle Leader head harness. (Photo courtesy of Premiere Pet Products, LLC.)

tip 59. Plan special treats

One of the challenges of working with a dog outside is that we're competing with such wonderful things—other dogs, wildlife, strange humans, untold interesting sights and smells.

One way we can compete with all this is to use extra special treats. Trainers refer to this as the *value* of a reward. For instance, I use plain old kibble to train my dog when we're indoors. But outside, if anything exciting is going on, she may not even notice a piece of kibble if I hold it in front of her nose!

So find treats that will grab your dog's attention. Small amounts of commercial training treats, particularly strong-smelling formulas like those containing liver, are one idea. Cheese, bits of hot dog, or bits of hamburger are also possibilities. (Note that although many trainers use people food for treats, you have to use good judgment! Don't overdo a new type of treat right away, until you're sure it won't upset your dog's digestion. Take care that your treats aren't throwing your dog's diet out of balance. Check with a trusted veterinarian if you're unsure what treats to use.)

Chapter 7

Recall

For those times when your dog is not safely inside, or on a leash, having a good recall behavior is essential. Recall means that your dog comes to you when you call. It can be a challenging behavior to train, but the tips in this section will help.

A key foundation behavior for training a recall is attention. Reward your dog consistently for "checking in" with you, and for looking at you when you say her name.

tip 60. Make attention the foundation of your recall

If your dog is going to *come* when called, she has to *notice* you've called. She has to be paying attention to you. So one foundation for training a recall is to teach your dog to pay attention to you—to "check in" with you regularly and often, and to notice when you ask her for attention.

Fortunately, this is a simple behavior to practice. Just reward your dog for paying attention to you. Suppose you have a puppy and she's been playing with a toy but suddenly drops it and comes over to say hi. Give her a treat or a nice scratch behind the ears.

Reward your dog for checking in with you in the backyard, or for looking for you when you've been out of sight for a while.

Another good idea is to reward your dog for responding to her name. Say her name before you put down her supper dish, or hand her a new toy. Toss her treats if you say her name and she looks at you.

Practice taking your dog's collar while giving him treats. This helps prevent him from learning to shy away when you reach for his collar—an important part of successfully collecting your dog when you've called him.

tip 61. Start training recall indoors

One of the things that makes recalls challenging is that we expect it to work outside—and outside is a high-distraction environment.

Have you ever been reading, or watching television, and someone has said something to you—but you didn't hear? Or maybe you realized they spoke, but didn't understand what was said?

When we pay attention to one thing, we often block out everything else. Dogs do this, too. And when a dog is outside, he's got a lot to pay attention to! For this reason, it's best to begin training recalls in a space that has few distractions—like your kitchen, or living room, or even a bathroom.

Reward your dog every time she comes to you when called. Waiting for a sit will also train your dog to ask for rewards politely, like these two are doing.

tip 62. Reward consistently

Make sure that you *always* make it rewarding for your dog to come when you've called. For that matter, make it rewarding for your dog to come up to you and check in, even if you haven't called. By doing this, you reinforce that coming to you means good things—every time.

tip 63. Make the reward for coming *wonderful*

Along with distractions, another reason recalls can be hard to train is that running around outside is tremendously rewarding to your dog. Depending on where you are, your dog may be playing with other dogs, or smelling interesting smells, or just stretching her legs after a dull day indoors. The things a loose dog finds to do can be really, really *fun*.

You need to make it even more rewarding for your dog to come to you. How do you do this? It depends on your dog. Since food is almost universally rewarding to dogs, many trainers suggest using food treats. However, make sure you pick the right treat. When you're competing against other rewards, it's best to use a high value treat—something really special. Examples include a bit of cheese, a chunk of hot dog, or a liver treat. You want to teach your dog that next time she has a choice to make, it's best to choose you—because you are more rewarding than whatever else is going on.

Play is sometimes a great reward as well. Does your dog like to chase balls? Offer a game of fetch as a reward for coming when called.

The important thing is to know your dog and to know what is rewarding to her. Be creative. Make coming when called the most rewarding thing that's happening to your dog *at that moment in time.*

tip 64. Use dinnertime as recall practice

Want a great way to get in some recall practice? Call your dog at dinner-time, every time. Do this even if he's standing on your toes while you're filling his dish. Say his name and your recall word (such as, "Come") and then set his dish down. *Voila:* instant recall practice!

tip 65. **Always use your "happy voice" for recalls!**

How do *you* like being called? Do you like the person calling you to sound angry or stressed? Or do you like being called by someone who sounds happy?

A dog who's been consistently rewarded for coming when called will run to you enthusiastically.

When we use an angry, frustrated, or stressed-out voice to call our dogs, we aren't making the recall as rewarding as we should. Use a happy tone of voice to communicate that coming to you is fun.

Sometimes, after you've called your dog, let him go play some more. This shows your dog that a recall doesn't always mean playtime is over.

tip 66. Never practice calling your dog unless you're sure he is going to come

With recalls, the last thing you want is to teach your dog to tune you out. Yet many people do this without realizing it. The trick is to make sure that, when you practice recalls, every attempt ends in success.

Especially at first, you should only call your dog when he is already on his way to you. If your dog is merrily running in the other direction, and you're shouting at him to come, you're not training the behavior you want. Instead, he's practicing to regard your yells as background noise.

Here, my Corgi has heard my voice—notice her ears have swiveled back to listen to me— which makes it more likely that she'll respond to my cue if I call her.

Here's where your work observing your dog pays off. Watch his body language. You'll notice that sometimes he'll seem intensely interested in something he's seen, heard, or smelled. When he is, the risk that he won't come when called is a lot greater. Other times, you'll notice he doesn't seem too interested in what's around him. Maybe he's even looked at you to see what you're doing. Call him now, and chances are much better that he'll come. And you'll be practicing the recall behavior you want.

If your dog's attention is fully focused on something besides you—like another dog—and you suspect he won't come if called, *don't call him.* All you'll accomplish is to give him practice at not coming. Wait until he's lost interest in the distraction or has voluntarily checked in with you, then practice your recall cue.

tip 67. Punishment can backfire!

One of the worst things people do when they are trying to train recalls is to punish a dog who hasn't come right away. Think about it. Your dog takes off up the street. You call her. She doesn't hear you. Or maybe she does hear you, but she's having too much fun to come to you.

Finally, you manage to catch up to her and get your hand on her collar. If you punish her now, you'll only teach her one thing: that letting you catch her results in bad things.

So, no matter how frustrated you are, no matter how embarrassing it is to be seen running after your dog, no matter how upset or angry you feel, you must always, always make your dog glad when she is finally back near you again.

tip 68. Don't take risks

Experienced trainers know better than to risk their dogs' lives on their recalls. They know that, no matter how well a dog is trained, things can go wrong. So if you are outdoors with your dog in a situation that is dangerous—where he might be hit by a car, for example, or be lost or injured—keep him on a leash.

tip 69. Manage your expectations

Don't expect your dog to have a solid recall overnight. Mastering this behavior takes time. Plan to measure your dog's progress over months, even years. That way you'll avoid getting frustrated and will be able to focus on your dog's successes.

tip 70. In an emergency—do anything that works!

Training a recall is challenging. It takes time, and even a well-trained dog might not respond to the recall cue every single time you use it. So what do you do if your dog won't respond to your cue? What if, for example, your dog gets loose, by accident, in a strange place? Here are some things you can try.

- Make a lot of silly noises—loud, silly, excited noises—and run away from your dog. Pretend you're chasing something or that you've found something your dog will find very interesting or exciting.

- Try a word that your dog associates with treats or meals. If you always say, "Cookies" when you open your dog's treat jar, try saying, "Cookies!" If you always say, "Ready for your dinner?" at mealtimes, try that.

- Try saying, "Sit" or "Down". If you've done lots of repetitions of these behaviors, your dog might drop into a sit or down, giving you an opportunity to get your hand on her collar.

- Toss your leash. If you can get close enough, gently toss your leash so that it touches your dog. The intention is not to hurt her, but to turn her attention away from whatever she's doing (chasing a squirrel or sniffing at the neighborhood dogs' marking spots) so you have a chance to get within arm's distance.

While these tricks might work once, or even two or three times, they may lose their power if overused. So be sure to work on your recall training, and only use these techniques if you don't have any other options, or if your dog might be in danger.

And be sure to reward your dog with lots of treats and pets when you have her back under your control—even if you used a trick to get her to come, instead of your recall cue.

Bonus tip: Train a backup recall cue

Some people train a backup recall cue. The purpose of this cue is to have another tool for absolute emergencies—if your dog is heading toward a busy highway, for example, or a potentially dangerous wild animal. It works a lot like saying, "Cookies!" or, "Dinnertime!"—only you set it up deliberately as a backup recall cue.

First, pick a word that you seldom use in normal conversation, like "Eureka." Then, several times a week, say that word, and when you do, give your dog a really fabulous food reward. The food should be high value (something the dog really loves) and there should be enough of it that it takes your dog thirty seconds or so to eat it all.

Finally, never, ever use the word without pairing it with this extra special treat—*unless* it is a real emergency and you don't happen to have extra special treats with you.

Chapter 8

Around Other Dogs and People

Chances are your dog will spend a lot of time with you. But he's also likely to come into contact with other people, and, of course, other dogs. Ideally, when these situations occur your dog will be confident and won't exhibit inappropriate aggression or fear. This section includes tips to help you train your dog to be comfortable in social situations.

tip 71. Start early

Trainers and behaviorists generally agree that dogs begin learning many responses when they are still puppies. So if you want your dog to be comfortable around other dogs and other people, you need to get started right from puppyhood.

tip 72. Give your puppy new experiences...

It's important to get your puppy desensitized to a variety of experiences so that he's used to all the many sights, sounds, smells, and other sensations that he's likely to encounter at some point in his life.

The process, which people sometimes refer to as *socialization*, should include exposure to different surroundings (such as city streets, parks, waterfront locations, public buildings, various rooms in your house) and noises (lawnmowers, vacuum cleaners, motorcycles, children playing).

Give your puppy an opportunity to walk on different kinds of surfaces and observe a variety of moving vehicles, from bicycles and scooters to buses and trains.

You should also get your puppy used to a variety of people. Expose your dog to people of different ages and ethnic backgrounds, who may wear different styles of dress. Try to get your dog used to seeing people with umbrellas and people in wheelchairs.

tip 73. ...but make sure your dog is *always* comfortable

Exposing your puppy or dog to a variety of experiences is very important. But you must make sure the experience is a positive one for your dog.

It helps to bear in mind that your dog is always learning. Therefore, anytime she has a nice, rewarding time, she's learning to be more calm and confident. If, on the other hand, she becomes uncomfortable, you risk teaching her something else. She may learn that certain things or people are scary, unpleasant, or even dangerous.

Watch your dog. Use your understanding of her body language to tell if she's relaxed, or aroused, or anxious. If she ever seems too anxious, or if she shows signs of fear or aggressiveness, that's a sign that you've pushed her too far, too fast.

This is particularly important if your dog is on the timid side. Some dogs are inherently more confident than others. If your dog tends to be underconfident, take special care in exposing her to other dogs and people. Pushing a timid dog too fast can make her fearfulness become worse, instead of better.

tip 74. Pick the right playmate

Most dogs love to play with other dogs. But make sure you pick the right playmate. When you introduce your dog to others, watch them play. If they are a good match, neither dog will become overly aroused or anxious.

Signs of an anxious dog include trembling, sweaty paw pads, tense muscles, tense mouth, dilated pupils, drooling, running away, hiding, and repetitive behaviors like whining or licking. When an anxious dog barks, it's likely to be higher pitched.

An aroused dog might have raised hackles, pricked ears, or an erect tail (or some combination). An aroused dog might also bark or growl.

tip 75. Don't overdo playtime

Have you ever stayed at a party too long—and instead of being fun, it started to feel stressful? Sometimes dogs can also have too much of a good thing. Even if your dog loves to play with his doggy buddies, don't overdo it. This is especially important if your dog tends to become overly excited or aroused. A good rule of thumb: end playtime while your dog is still having fun.

tip 76. Manage the people, too

Sometimes, to keep your dog comfortable around people, you have to train the people.

For instance, never let a person frighten your dog. If you have company come to your house, don't let people crowd your dog, or force him to have contact with them, if he shows signs of being anxious about it.

When you are out on walks, don't let strangers approach your dog inappropriately. Make sure they understand your rules for how your dog is approached and petted. If your rule is that people should only pet your dog on the head, for example, communicate that to people so that someone doesn't grab your dog in a hug.

It can be difficult for amateur dog trainers to interpret dog behavior. However, researchers like Turid Rugaas (see Additional Reading for more information) have helped people understand how dogs communicate with one another using body language. The dog on the right is using two signals described by Rugaas—licking his lips and looking away—to show the other dog that he doesn't want a confrontation.

tip 77. If you think it's aggression— get help

Most of the time, we're able to handle dog training ourselves. But sometimes we should consult an experienced professional. In particular, if your dog is showing aggression toward people (for example, snapping, nipping, or baring her teeth), you should consult a behaviorist or professional trainer.

Many dogs will occasionally exhibit some of these behaviors toward other dogs. It can be a useful way for dogs to communicate—a way of saying, "Hey, give me my space."

But sometimes, dogs learn to use these behaviors inappropriately. If you have concerns, getting a second opinion from a professional can help you better understand your dog's behavior.

Chapter 9

If Things Go Wrong

Professional dog trainers spend their lives learning how to train dogs. They clock hours and hours of time observing dogs, training dogs, learning what works and what doesn't. Yet even professional dog trainers are sometimes stumped. So don't be dismayed if your training doesn't seem to be working as well as you'd like all the time.

Usually, the setback is just temporary. Dogs have "off days" just like people do. Other times, we may need to adjust our training, or try a different approach. Here are some tips to help you if things go wrong and you need to get your training program back on track.

tip 78. Take a break

Sometimes, the best thing to do when your dog training hits a rough spot is to stop for a while. Wait until you feel less stressed. A break can sometimes give you the perspective you need to figure out how you can change your training program to get better results.

tip 79. Back up to something easier

Sometimes our training goes wrong because we've asked too much of our dogs. Take leash walking, for example. Suppose your dog walks beautifully on leash—as long as you're walking around your backyard. The minute you go out onto the sidewalk, however, she acts as if she's never practiced loose leash walking in her life.

The solution: back up. For the next span of time—a few more days, maybe even a week or more—stick to practicing in your backyard again. By grooving in that loose leash behavior a little more, your dog will be better prepared for a more challenging environment—so next time, you may find she's able to succeed.

tip 80. **Schedule a vet exam**

If you observe sudden changes in your dog's temperament or behavior patterns, don't overlook the possibility that the trigger is some sort of injury or medical condition. For instance, if your dog was housebroken but suddenly starts urinating indoors, definitely schedule a vet check.

tip 81. Look for causes

When we hit a dead end with training our dogs, it's easy to focus on the problem. But it's better to look for the cause. Doing that will make you better equipped to respond.

For example, suppose you have a problem with your dog digging holes in the yard. It is helpful to figure out what is triggering the digging. Perhaps your dog has too much energy and digging is a way to burn it off. If that's the case, giving your dog more exercise might reduce the digging behavior. Repetitive behaviors sometimes indicate anxiety. A dog who becomes anxious when left alone for too long might start doing destructive things like digging (if left outside), or chewing, or scratching (if left inside). For this dog, addressing the separation issues would alleviate the digging.

It can also be helpful to review theory. Give yourself a brush-up course on behavior modification. Perhaps you'll discover a fresh idea or insight that will help you become a better trainer and overcome the roadblock you've faced.

tip 82. Consult an expert

If you're really stumped—or if you feel truly overwhelmed by the problem you've encountered—consider getting help from a qualified trainer or behaviorist. This tip is particularly important if your problem involves aggressive displays, such as baring teeth, air snapping, nipping, or biting.

tip 83. Try something new!

When you run into an impasse with your dog, maybe it's time to throw out everything you've tried so far and start over with something completely new. Check the Internet, read a book, or talk to a dog-loving friend. The neat new idea you try might just be the one that works.

Chapter 10

Problem Chewing

Dogs love to chew—and puppies love to chew even more. Use the tips in this chapter to keep your dog's chewing behavior from eating you out of house and home.

tip 84. Keep chew toys around

One of the best ways to prevent problem chewing is to give your dog chew toys. That way she'll have a positive outlet for her chewing behavior.

tip 85. Pick safe toys

Make sure your dog's chew toys are safe. Avoid toys that come apart: your dog may swallow pieces. Don't leave your dog alone with a chew toy unless you're certain it will hold up.

Some dogs are stronger, more persistent chewers than others, so a chew toy that works for one dog may not work for another. And even a durable chew toy may fall apart with age, so periodically inspect your dog's chew toys to make sure they're still intact.

There are chew products that are made to be ingested. Experiment with these, and if they don't upset your dog's digestion, they might be a good option.

If your dog is a chewer (and that means most puppies!) keep an eye on her around objects, like sticks, that might come apart.

After my dog broke two teeth on "marrow bone" chew toys, my vet recommended pigs' hooves. My dog loves them. They are tough enough that large pieces don't easily break off, but not quite as hard as bone.

tip 86. Vary toys for interest

Dogs can get bored with the same old chew toys. Keep a variety of toys on hand and rotate them so your dog has a "new" toy every few days.

tip 87. Reward appropriate chewing

Because dogs like to chew, the chewing itself is rewarding. But you can make it even more rewarding. When you see your dog chewing something you want her to chew, say, "Yes" and give her a treat. This tip is especially useful for puppies and young dogs, when you're working to get good chewing habits established.

It's important to prevent your dog from getting into the habit of chewing things he shouldn't!

tip 88. Prevent mistakes

Bad chewing habits are just that—habits. So it's important to prevent bad habits from getting started. If you have a puppy or young dog, or a dog who is new to your household, don't leave him unsupervised. If he starts getting used to chewing something he shouldn't, it will be that much harder to train him to chew appropriately.

tip 89. Don't turn bad chewing into a game!

If you do catch your dog chewing something she shouldn't, it's best not to show a reaction. Hand her a chew toy to work on instead. If you appear to become excited by her chewing, you may accidentally teach her that she can chew certain things to get your attention.

tip 90. Consider adding extra exercise

Sometimes dogs chew because it helps them burn off excess energy. So if your dog is chewing inappropriately, ask yourself how much exercise he's getting. Or try increasing his exercise and see if that helps alleviate the chewing behavior.

tip 91. Talk "dog" to a mouthing puppy

Sometimes the thing getting chewed by your dog isn't your stuff. Sometimes it's you. Puppies use their mouths to play. But they also have to learn how hard they can bite without causing their playmates distress. As it turns out, they have a great way of teaching this to each other. If a puppy gets a bit too rough with a playmate, the playmate yips. This shows the puppy that his bites are too hard. If the yip doesn't stop the too-rough behavior, the playmate will end the game and move away.

You can communicate to your puppy in the same way. Suppose your puppy is playing with you and starts mouthing your hand too hard. When you feel too much pressure, give a short, high-pitched "yipe!" and stop playing for a second. If the puppy doesn't stop playing—if he continues to try to mouth you—fold your arms and turn away. Or get up and walk away for a few minutes until your puppy has had a chance to calm down.

Playing is very rewarding for puppies. This technique uses play as a reward to teach your puppy to mouth gently.

Chapter 11

Problem Barking

All dogs bark. But when a dog barks too much, it can cause problems. It can make the dog's human companions feel stressed. It can bother neighbors.

One difficulty with problem barking is determining how much barking is too much. It's a subjective judgment. One person may find even occasional barking irritating. Another person may be able to tune out the most incessant barker.

But if your dog's barking does seem to be creating problems, the tips in this section will help you modify that behavior.

tip 92. Figure out the trigger

Dogs bark for different reasons, depending on the dogs and the circumstances. If your dog barks excessively, the first thing you need to do is figure out what's triggering the barking.

Pay attention to when your dog barks. Is it when you're home, or are your neighbors complaining that your dog barks when you are out? Is the barking happening outdoors or inside?

Does the barking seem to be triggered by things your dog sees or hears? Animals in the yard? People walking by the house? Or does your dog appear to bark for no reason?

Sometimes you can find clues in the other behaviors that accompany the barking. A dog who sits at your feet and barks at you is barking for a different reason (perhaps for attention) than a dog who barks while looking out windows.

Once you know the trigger, you may be able to eliminate it. For example, suppose a birdfeeder in your backyard attracts squirrels, and your dog barks out the window when the squirrels come by to eat. Perhaps you can reposition the feeder so that the squirrels aren't as visible from your house.

Knowing the trigger may also help you modify the barking behavior, because you'll be able to anticipate it. For instance, if your dog barks when the mailman arrives, you can work on training your dog to choose a different behavior at those times. Examples of alternate behaviors include sitting, picking up a toy, or performing some trick like rolling over—anything that causes your dog to stop barking.

tip 93. Avoid a bored dog

One reason some dogs bark is boredom. If you suspect this is why your dog barks, make sure she isn't left alone, for too long, with nothing to do. This is particularly true if you work outside the home and your dog is left by herself for many hours a day. Leave her some chew toys. Arrange to come home during the day to take her for a walk.

tip 94. Consider a dog walker or doggy day care

If your dog is barking when you're away at work, consider having a dog walker or pet sitter come to your home to give your dog some attention and exercise. Or consider doggy day care. By providing your dog with exercise and companionship, you'll help eliminate the root cause of the barking.

tip 95. Train an alternative behavior

If your dog barks at specific triggers—like the arrival of the mail, or critters in your backyard—try training an alternative behavior. Pick one that makes it hard, if not impossible, for your dog to bark.

For example, suppose your dog barks at guests at the door. Try training your dog to pick up a toy when guests arrive. Most dogs find it harder to bark with their mouths full!

tip 96. Meet your dog halfway

Dogs bark. Therefore, when we invite them into our lives, we're bound to get some barking in our lives as well. And in fact, their barking can be helpful. Dogs have more sensitive hearing and smell than humans do. Their barking can alert us to things that we cannot sense.

So try to keep your dog's barking in perspective. At the very least, by accepting *some* barking in your life, you'll keep yourself from going too crazy.

Chapter 12

Attitude and Perspective

We make dogs our companions because of the way they make us feel. Our relationships with our dogs inspire us to feel love, contentment, and a connection to something greater than ourselves. So when it comes to modifying our dogs' behavior, we need to also keep the right attitude and perspective.

Spending time with your dog is one of life's greatest pleasures. So keep your training upbeat and remember to enjoy your dog.

tip 97. Have fun!

Working with your dog should be an upbeat, happy experience. So whatever goals you set for yourself, have fun working toward them!

tip 98. Don't be hard on your dog

No dog is born perfectly trained. It takes time and effort to elicit and reinforce the behaviors you want in your dog. And chances are pretty good that you may hit some bumps in the road on the way.

If you do, don't get frustrated with your dog. It's not his fault. Take a deep breath, take a break, and try again later when you feel more relaxed.

tip 99. Don't be hard on yourself

Some of us blame ourselves for our dog's behavior. You do need to take responsibility for your dog. But at the same time, keep a balanced perspective. Don't punish yourself if you are falling short of the training goals you've set.

tip 100. Remember the big picture

Having a dog around is a wonderful experience. We love that doggy grin when we return home after an absence. We love our dog's eagerness when it's time for a walk. We love that wet nose pushing into our hand when our dog wants to be petted.

Moreover, even the most challenging dog gets some things right! It's helpful to remember our many successes with our dog and to keep our occasional frustrations in perspective.

tip 101. Reward yourself, too!

Dogs aren't the only creatures who deserve rewards when they do well. People do, too. So don't forget to reward yourself. Take pride in the achievements you realize by working with your dog. Notice how much better you are today, as a trainer, than you were in the past.

Then do something nice for yourself. You've earned it!

Training your dog can be challenging and requires a lot of effort on your part. So don't forget to reward yourself, too. You deserve it!

Additional Reading

Alexander, Melissa C., and Robert Bailey. *Click for Joy! Questions and Answers from Clicker Trainers and Their Dogs.* Waltham (Mass.): Sunshine Books, 2003.

Brown, Ali. *Scaredy Dog! Understanding and Rehabilitating Your Reactive Dog.* Allentown (Penn.): Tanacacia Press, 2004.

Coppinger, Raymond, and Lorna Coppinger. *Dogs: A Startling New Understanding of Canine Origin, Behavior and Evolution.* New York: Scribner, 2001.

Donaldson, Jean. *Culture Clash.* Berkeley (Calif.): James & Kenneth Publishers, 1997.

King, Trish. *Parenting Your Dog.* Neptune (N.J.): TFH Publications, 2004.

McConnell, Patricia. *The Other End of the Leash.* New York: Ballantine Books, 2003.

Miller, Pat, and Jean Donaldson. *The Power of Positive Dog Training.* New York: Howell Book House, 2001.

Pryor, Karen. *Don't Shoot the Dog! The New Art of Teaching and Training.* New York: Bantam Books, 1999.

Rugaas, Turid. *On Talking Terms With Dogs: Calming Signals.* Wenatchee (Wash.): Dogwise Publishing; 2nd edition, 2005.

Ryan, Terry, and Kirsten Mortensen. *Outwitting Dogs.* Guilford (Conn.): The Lyons Press, 2004.

Yin, Sophia. *How to Behave So Your Dog Behaves.* Neptune (N.J.): TFH Publications, 2004.